WEEDING
WITHOUT
CHEMICALS

WEEDING WITHOUT CHEMICALS

·Bob Flowerdew·

Kyle Cathie Limited

This paperback edition published in Great
Britain in 2018 by Kyle Cathie Limited
Part of Octopus Publishing Group Limited
Carmelite House, 50 Victoria Embankment
London EC4Y 0SZ
www.kylebooks.co.uk

First published in hardback in 2010

Text 2010 © Bob Flowerdew
Design 2010 © Kyle Cathie Limited
Photography 2010 © Peter Cassidy
Illustration 2010 © Alison Clements

ISBN 978-0-85783-471-3

10 9 8 7 6 5 4 3 2 1

A Cataloguing in Publication record for this title
is available from the British Library.

Photography: Peter Cassidy
Illustrations: Alison Clements
Design: Louise Leffler
Project Editor: Sophie Allen
Copy Editor: Helena Caldon

Photographic Acknowledgements:
All photography by Peter Cassidy except
pp. 77, 79, 98 by Frank Yorke

Printed in China by 1010 Printing Ltd

Contents

Introduction

The classic definition of a weed is a plant in the wrong place. And, to be fair, that is about it. Any plant may become a weed if it's vigorously invasive or good at self-seeding. Many of our common weeds were once grown as garden flowers, and some as vegetables. We may tolerate some prettier weeds (wild flowers) in certain areas but in most parts of the garden they must be barred or they can soon take over.

A weed may be itself unsightly or merely blocking the view of other prettier plants. It may, if left, keep on spreading and become more than an inconvenience. A motley host of weeds compete with our chosen plants for nutrients, water, light and air, but worse, weeds support, overwinter, encourage and spread pests and diseases. So weeds have to be controlled or even eradicated; that is much of the work of gardening.

Although almost any plant could become a weed by doing too well in the wrong place, most 'weeds' are those annoying green things that come up everywhere; between our cherished plants, through the hedge and springing along the cracks in paving. We don't know all their names but we soon get to know the look of them well enough.

This book is about how to simply and easily control these weeds – and how to do so with little effort, ecological intrusion or cost.

Right: Dead nettles; weed or ground cover under these raspberries?

What are weeds?

A weed is, indeed, well-defined as a plant in the wrong place. One cannot put it better. In another spot or time, the same plant would be a native benefiting insect life, a ground stabiliser, a nutrient recycler or even a garden flower, but right now, where it is, it is unwanted, thus a weed. Another way of putting it is: 'If it multiplies fast, is not choosy as to soil, shade or situation, is immune to most pests and diseases, then if it's not a weed already it soon will be.'

Left: There is little easier to maintain than a bed of weeds
Right: In another time or place, a weed may become an esteemed flower

Many of our garden flowers have moved out to become vagrant weeds, albeit relatively pretty ones. The story is often told of the rosebay willowherb, once admired as a garden plant, for the flowers supposedly resembled those of the tender rosebay or oleander. It then became a plague when the steam railroad provided burnt-off areas where the windborne fluffy seeds could alight and take over. The sides of the tracks still carry many dense patches of this delightful invader. Many train travellers around England are also rewarded by the massive flower show, apparently deliberately sown, of countless buddleias. Indeed, the former are such prolific seeders that almost every derelict urban garden or wasteground has its buddleias taking over. It is remarkable considering the original purple form was not introduced from China until 1890; it is claimed the bombsites of World War II enabled this plant to multiply. The sycamore is an older escapee, long naturalised and still a perpetual weed problem to neighbours. Evening primroses are one of the newer weeds, appearing with delightful big yellow flowers at dusk all summer, and multiplying relentlessly. Canadian fleabane has no known good attributes and is silently taking over most of Europe. You will soon know it.

Any plant that just won't stop growing is a weed, to all intents. A neighbour's giant leylandi hedge on your once sunny side could be looked at as a huge weed problem, though that is no compensation. Likewise, climbers too vigorous for their original support can become weeds to everything else – rambling roses are notorious. However, most weed control is concerned with much smaller stuff.

'Ancient Greek myths were likely the result of "Chinese whispers" and "Fisherman's tales" thus such foes as the many headed hydra were based on the real reports of prospective settlers encountering bindweed!'

Right: There's never a weed in the frame yet each was from where it came

Why weeds appear

Almost every spoonful of soil has enough seeds in it to cover a very large area with growing things; some of which may be pretty, but the majority will be 'just' weeds. The exact mix depends on the soil qualities and, as importantly, its history. For fairly obvious reasons, acid soil has acid-loving weeds, chalky soil, lime lovers, and in damp shade you do not find many weeds of arid, sun-scorched, stony sites. Weeds growing in a place show you the conditions they like – if they were not experiencing these, they would not be thriving there as weeds.

Right: Goosegrass and stinging nettles compete for this space; both are fast growing so it's going to be a close race

Many seeds arrive on the wind, and not just tiny fluffy ones
- ash and sycamore keys may travel miles

But the ancestors of those weeds had to find those spots in the first place, so sometimes the weeds in a soil may also tell us something of what has taken place there in the past. Masses of stinging nettles are almost always a sign of old human habitations, as they love the rich sites made by our relentless dumping of garbage and wastes. In East Anglia, the angelica-like alexanders is a rare roadside weed found only near old Roman habitation sites. Many docks indicate that a field has probably been used for pasturing horses, as the seeds pass through a horse undigested, or it may, of course, just show that the soil had some horse manure applied to it.

Other weeds blow in on the breeze; these may even be quite large, such as ash and sycamore keys. Seeds as large as acorns and hazelnuts can be blown by gales, and, of course, squirrels bury nuts. All are valuable trees in the right place but in your flower or vegetable bed – a weed. Under trees, shrubs and other perching places, bird droppings soon give rise to all sorts of weeds from the berries and seeds the birds have eaten. We can also import weed seeds or even whole specimens on top of the compost of pot-grown plants from unscrupulous garden centres. Hairy bitter cress was unknown before the pot plant boom, now it's almost everywhere.

Where weeds

come from

Weeds are the way in which nature heals the green covering of this earth. Many are the re-coverers when a bare piece of soil appears; as after a landfall, when a large tree is uprooted, a mole hill, a badger or rabbit digs a den, or when a shallow wet area becomes muddy and dry. All these bits of loose earth need fixing to stop the soil washing or blowing away, thus seeds that have survived a long time buried or are blown in on the wind are going to be the first to cover the ground. Left to themselves, the first settlers eventually change the conditions, and by covering the soil surface they leave little bare earth for themselves to seed into, so very soon more enduring perennial plants take over.

In most temperate zones, the final result is a deciduous forest and it would take your average back garden a surprisingly small amount of time to get there. Left to itself, most ground will soon become dominated by grasses, nettles and thistles, then by brambles and briars and shrubs – themselves to be later replaced or rather overgrown by tree saplings. It does not matter much whether the ground starts as bare soil, turf, rockery, shrubbery or driveway; within a matter of decades it can be covered by trees, perhaps with an understorey of shade-tolerant shrubs and plants that grow close to the ground, such as ivy.

Thus, much of gardening is really about arresting nature's inevitable progression. The further back you want to halt the process, the harder it is to maintain. Fill an area with huge trees or shrubs and they will choke out most other plants – though even here there is always a weed or two that may creep in, such as bindweed, bryony or old man's beard. Try to keep bare soil between rows of vegetables or bedding plants and you will be relentlessly fighting legions of weeds that spring back, hydra-like, every time you strike them down.

Left: Brambles soon take over an area - but are themselves replaced by trees in only a decade or three

'A year's seeds, seven years of weeds'

Potential weeds are all round our gardens, invading with roots, stems, and seeds. It is the latter that are the hosts waiting in reserve to replace all the others we deal with. Once we clear a bed of nettles, ten thousand seedlings appear. Clear them and another legion appear; and so on, in perpetuity. This is especially so if we do not weed persistently and regularly and, to some extent, thoughtfully.

Those species that manage to hide and set seed despite our sporadic weeding attempts will become our most often found weeds. The poppies of Flanders turned the shelled and blasted mud to crimson because that land had poppies growing amongst corn for centuries before. Their seed was everywhere, and being both fast-growing and fast-maturing, poppies soon proliferated, but once grasses and other plants returned, the poppies were edged out to only appear in the corn or where the soil was disturbed again.

The old saying is 'a year's seeds, seven years of weeds', but seven years will not get rid of all the potential weeds, only the majority. Turn over the soil from a long-covered piece of ground, say under a wooden shed, and there will soon be nightshades and other long-lived seeds germinating – some may live for centuries. So this saying is a huge understatement; most weeds left to go to seed will provide a residue of little seedlings to appear every time the soil is disturbed, not just for seven, but for many more years. Some seed will stay dormant for decades, or much longer, and only germinate when the conditions change. Say when an old hedge is removed: the faster germinating and more quickly setting weeds soon spread their seeds thickly around, proliferate and leave a fund of seeds for the next opportunity. Their very

Left: Poppies are weeds of tilled land, simply because their rapid cycle from seed to seed again fits within that of our crops

speed betters their chance of survival, and this is why we see weeds come up before so many of our sown plants. Their ability to lie low for ages, then germinate and reproduce quickly is what effectively makes most plants weeds. Thus, slow-growing, rare to set seed alpines and orchids do not appear in anyone's list of weeds.

There are, of course, those other weeds that start from airborne invasion. From the stately, tall rosebay willowherb already mentioned, to the prostrate dandelion, with groundsel and thistles in between, all come on the wind and in droves or simply drop down from weeds nearby. We often make matters worse for ourselves; if we let anything, but especially known weeds, flower and set seed then we are asking for trouble. If you cannot get rid of the weeds, at least stop them multiplying by chopping their heads off. And knowingly planting known offenders, such as, say, pot marigolds, poppies, foxgloves or sycamores, next to a gravel drive or a pristine bed and letting them set seed is just plain foolish.

If we remove every weed and leave bare soil – and do nothing else for a couple of months – then the ground will become covered with weeds. Some of those weeds, such as bitter cress and chickweed, may actually germinate, grow, flower and set seed within that time. This ensures that the next occasion you expose or bare that soil, these weeds will now predominate even more – probably in thick mats this time. At least you will have fewer types of weed to worry about for a while, just masses of those faster ones, but this also means that to gain control, you will have to weed more often to get rid of all those fresh flushes of seedlings.

Sporadic weeding means more weeds, for although you cannot easily get rid of all the seeds in your soil, only those in the topmost layer tend to germinate. Now, regular frequent weeding not only gets rid of the weed seedlings from old seed but stops new seed being added back. Thus, slowly, your topmost layer of soil can become relatively easy to keep weed free, as most of the seeds likely to germinate will eventually have done so. A regularly hoed rose bed can soon be little work to hoe, but if instead this is done only now and again it will become a difficult and burdensome task. Truly, every gardener gets the weeds they deserve, as well as those they inherit!

Right: Such a glorious flower, and what an invasive seed head to come

Why weed and when?

Well, as previously mentioned, we weed for a whole load of reasons; mostly because we sort of know it has to be done, but different weeds need removing for more specific reasons, as well as because they are being generally troublesome. Thornapples (datura) are so competitive for phosphate they can make a soil almost infertile; shepherd's purse is closely related to brassicas (the cabbage family) and spreads many of their problem pests and diseases; while brambles, briars and stinging nettles just become awkward to evict if given any time to establish.

Actually, timing is everything and, as you get to know your plants and weeds, you learn when weeding is crucially important, and when it is only urgent. Small seedling crops or bedding plants cannot outgrow a flush of almost any weeds and are soon choked by them; bigger stronger plants only suffer minor losses by comparison, or almost none at all. A crop of full-grown onions may actually benefit from a flush of young weeds taking up spare nitrogen and water, which helps them ripen. Grass and clover in an established orchard become not weeds but ground cover; though weeds underneath a young tree, even many paces from its trunk, can still significantly reduce its growth.

Right: Shepherd's purse, so-called from the shape of its seeds, which are more like hearts, is such a pretty weed

It really is to reduce competition for water, air, light and nutrients that we must control weeds. The aesthetics, or lack of them, with a weedy bed counts for more in the flower garden, though weeds there are rarely fatal. But weed competition with crops is a more serious matter: crops need everything in good supply to perform well, while 'flowers' may even bloom more profusely with some competition.

Weeds are weeds often simply because they can grow faster than other plants in the same situation or can out-compete them for various necessities. Weeds are very wasteful of water and removing them means more for our plants. They even compete for carbon dioxide, which, although too plentiful worldwide in the upper atmosphere, is often scarce at plant level down near the ground. All too well do weeds compete for light – we all know how plants get drawn up and even shaded out by a choking mat of weeds around them. What we often don't notice, though, is the world of mineral competition. Many weeds are exceptionally good at scavenging for elements they need; some accumulate some elements to high levels, while at the same time depriving our plants of these scarce resources. However, once transferred to the compost heap or just rotted in situ, those elements become available again. Thus, a flush of weeds can be seen as a free source of fertility that just needs collecting or incorporating. So 'when to weed' becomes 'as often as possible', not just for control purposes but for maximum return. Certainly, hoeing, raking, smothering or incorporating a flush of weed seedlings returns a lot of fertility to the soil that was previously locked up in their seeds.

'Weed seeds are locked-up nutrients, weed seedlings are those nutrients free to be released once hoed under.'

Left: Weeds would be more competition than these early-into-leaf bulbs

And why not herbicides?

Those not wishing to be green and/or organic may wonder whether herbicides could be as useful to the gardener as they appear to be to many farmers. The first difference here is that the farmer is dealing with huge areas of monocrops and their herbicides are designed to kill everything else but the crop. This is not the same sort of situation as a garden with many different species all growing together. The use of herbicides on paths, drives and hard surfaces is more closely related to the agricultural situation and to some extent not so problematical. That is, provided no drift, run off or contamination occurs, and that the instructions for the herbicide are followed precisely. In practice, the weather makes a huge difference to the results and, unfortunately, the most difficult weeds are also almost immune to most herbicides.

Organic gardeners object to herbicides because they do not just kill the weeds but also hurt other living things they land on. Herbicides are also rather too often inadvertently insecticides, fungicides or nematicides, while many of the older ones have proven to have been avicides and mammalicides (going on to kill birds and animals). Most herbicides kill the microscopic plants, algae and much of the other flora and fauna on or in the soil and on plants. A further objection is that although an herbicide itself may or may not be an ecological disaster, the factory making it and all the associated by-products may well be.

But their principal drawback is that herbicides will not get rid of the really problem weeds when you need them to; particularly when the same weed, or even the same plant, is running widespread over several adjoining gardens. Many applications may be required to get only partial or temporary control of weeds, such as Japanese knotweed, bracken, bindweed or equisetum. These may still return after a short period of apparently successful elimination and. even if an established weed is totally eliminated, it may well have left seed to start thousands of new plants which now need to be dealt with. Although there are some herbicides that may prevent seed germination in bare soil, few now wish to use these amongst food crops or even in ornamental areas fearing, usually quite rightly, that they leave problematical residues.

Not the place to be throwing poisons around

Which weeds

There are a multitude of plants of all sorts of families and habits that could become weeds but, for convenience, they can mostly be grouped as a few fairly distinct groups of weed types. Those springing from seed are, to all intents and purposes, initially almost identical, regardless of whether they would eventually become annuals or perennials, soft or shrubby. Whilst small, they can be quickly and easily dealt with by hoeing, mulching, or a host of other methods. True, they will soon be replaced by another multitude springing from yet more seeds, and so on, for at least seven or more years but, none the less, all weeds coming from seed are relatively easily dealt with at this early stage.

Right: Groundsel flowers will rapidly be seeds and soon yet more groundsel

are worst?

When they become bigger, most weeds become much harder to eradicate. When hand weeding, you notice how soon some seedlings develop defences of prickles, thorns, and irritant sap. Weed soon and weed often is the easiest approach to eliminating these seedlings.

Now, as they get bigger, many go down the path of rapidly flowering and setting seed, particularly annuals such as groundsel. Some can even still set seed whilst lying uprooted and withering on the ground, if they have been allowed to reach any size. A few, such as hairy bitter cress, can create another generation in only a few weeks; most seed within the first growing year but many overwinter, flowering the next – but only if foolishly given the chance. Again, weeding soon and often is the best policy.

Weeds that establish for a year, building up reserves to then flower and seed the following year, are biennials such as evening primrose and foxgloves. They die once they have seeded, and so, because of this slower and self-eliminating habit, these plants are rarely a major weed problem unless they are allowed to be.

Other weeds prefer to dominate first then flower and seed, and these are mostly perennial weeds. Frequently, these are the weeds found on waste ground, as they take time to settle in but then hold on for a long time very tenaciously; they include stinging nettles, brambles and rosebay willowherb. Some of these are shrubby perennials which leave live woody bits above ground through winter, such as briars and brambles. Others are herbaceous and survive with tap roots, bulbs or other underground storage, such as thistles, docks, nettles and horseradish. Once established, these can be hard to eradicate as they regrow so well and so often. However, persistent weeding attacks will beat them every time, usually within the first year, occasionally longer.

But the real troublemakers are those with widely spreading root systems, such as bindweed, equisetum and bracken and, fortunately to a much lesser extent, stinging nettles, ivy, couch grass and ground elder. The first selection really are almost unbeatable unless you can control the area around your garden as well, otherwise they will just re-invade as fast as you remove any there already. The second group usually come in smaller patches, which can be attacked piecemeal and destroyed. Where they are on either side of a garden fence, barriers of plastic sheeting can be inserted in slit trenches to stop further incursions. Once isolated, the plant on

your side can be hacked to pieces enough times to kill it without much chance of recovery. Or you can join forces with your neighbours and eradicate both sides simultaneously.

Above: Foxgloves, as pretty as they are,
can self-seed their way to weedom

Weed identification

It really helps to know your weeds. If you don't yet know stinging nettles and annual meadow grass, you soon will. Others follow. It is relatively easy to know the common weeds when mature – docks, thistles, groundsel, dead nettles and so on – it takes a bit longer to recognise them at the seedling stage. None the less, they are all distinct. The grasses are soon obvious, though possibly confused with onion family weeds, which are fairly similar but usually distinctively smelly. The shape of dead nettle seedlings, the colour of dock seedlings, the first strands of chickweed; each becomes recognised and can be dealt with. Once your eye is in, you can spot unusual seedlings; this way many free plants can be had: yew, raspberry, blackberry, holly and other seed spread by birds come up all over a garden and can be saved from the weeding and potted up, if desired. Violets are common weeds, daphnes, bay laurel and honeysuckles much more seldom, but come up they sometimes do and they can be spared if spotted and recognised as such.

Left: A weedy mat of annual grasses is surface-rooting and thus easy to remove or incorporate

Weed sample ID

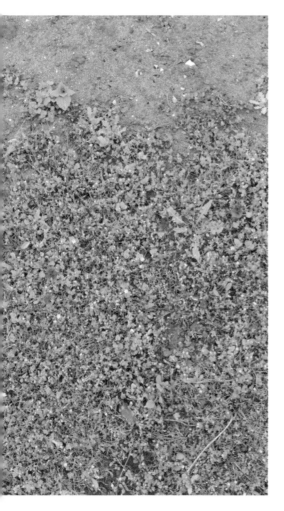

So here is how to easily learn to recognise the different weeds from when they are small. Take a seed tray or similar and fill it level with some sieved garden soil. Stand it in a tray of water to soak, then let it drain and stand it somewhere warm and sunny. A host of weed seedlings will appear. Remove the surplus multiple similar ones, leaving just two or three of each type you can tell apart. As these grow on some will soon become recognisable and nameable, these can now go. Eventually, most should become known, if not named, and maybe a couple of interesting plants may appear too, you never know.

Now you can do the same in the garden – just leave a small plot unweeded, watch the seedlings come up and, once again, thin down to a few of each type. Let them grow until you can recognise them. You don't really need to know their names; recognition is all that's important. Then they can be removed from amongst your sown seedlings with more ease and speed.

Above: A mass of weeds but nearly always the same ones in any place

Right: It doesn't help to know which exact weeds they are - as you can tell which are the carrots - but it helps to recognise them from early on

How to be rid of weeds — repetition and timing

The easy way is to simply remove each and every leaf each weekend. As I often quip: 'Try it with a houseplant and see how long that lives.' No plant can withstand losing all its leaves time and time again and faster than they can use sunlight to make more material. If the leaves are removed once monthly, take a week to regrow, and then have three weeks in the sun it is likely some plants could survive forever. However, destroy all leaves at least weekly and any new ones are then killed before they finish unfurling and so the plant must surely expire.

Repetition, repetition, repetition. Just keep doing it and the plant must eventually be weakened to the critical point and thereafter the exhausted roots wither away – but only if it's not being reinforced from somewhere else. Thus, it is important to first isolate the weed in question from any further clumps elsewhere. Obviously, in winter, growth is slower, so the gap between attacks need not be quite as close as in summer. Even so, the answer to effective weeding is to do it again and again, sooner rather than later, and then again and again until victory is yours. And, remember, the younger and smaller the weeds, the much easier they are to kill.

Right: Never stop weeding, as a weed will sneak in and multiply

There are some cases, though, when careful timing helps. Thistles are often best pulled as they start flowering and it is easiest to pull up stinging nettle roots in late winter, when they lose their grip on the soil. So if you want to clear a big patch of nettles in a new garden, clear their top growth in midwinter when it's all dried up and you can see hidden things such as wires and bricks. Then they can be dug up or their roots pulled in late winter. Any remaining shoots appearing in spring can be pulled and any seedlings hoed. (However, if, say, a patch of stinging nettles are wanted for compost material and you don't want to kill them off then you can cut or pull the tops two, three times or four every year and they will surely endure.)

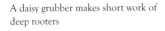

A daisy grubber makes short work of deep rooters

Weeding ways by hand

One of the most everyday of methods is to pull weeds up by their roots. Although effective this is not always a good idea. If the weeds are amongst other plants then their roots are intermeshed and pulling out the weeds may damage your plants' roots, which hurts established plants and may well be fatal to seedlings. But from bare soil or amongst robust, well-established plants, pulling may be allowable. When pulled, the weeds should be dropped into a bucket or trug straight away for composting and not left on the ground in case they re-root or drop seed. Also, do have a kneeling pad and gloves, because if you're comfortable you'll do a less rushed and better job.

Some weeds, especially those with a tap root, are hard to pull, such as docks and thistles. Often these are also rosette weeds in turf, such as plantains, thistles and dandelions. There is a special tool, called a daisy grubber, which levers these out most nicely. (Two prongs are pushed down either side of the weed and then levered up, pushing against a heel set just behind the prongs.)

An alternative to pulling is to detach the top from the roots with a knife as you pull. Many weeds will not regrow from their roots, a few will and so they might need a second or third decapitation. However, weeding with a knife is quick, clean and efficient, and you can even slice horizontally, severing many at a time. You could use a sharp-edged trowel to slice or scrape sideways; an onion or hand hoe may also be used like this. All these must be as sharp as razors; use a sharpening stone or a file to keep their edges keen – blunt tools do not work well or easily! Also, regularly clear any build up of fibres or soil on their edges.

Weeding ways standing up

Hoeing – This is using a sharp knife stuck on the end of a stick to cut weeds in half. A good hoe has a very long, smooth, light shaft and a light springy blade that's razor sharp. Most importantly, keep it sharp – blunt hoes do not work! There are many patterns of hoes in various shapes; one group being the chisel-like Dutch hoes which are shuffled to and fro through the topsoil. The other sort are swan-necked or draw hoes, with the head at near right angles to the shaft, which are used with a chopping or swinging action. This sort can also be used to draw soil up around stems. I'd avoid any patent hoe with moving parts, which won't move after a very short time, and I'd also avoid stainless steel or thick iron ones, because they are hard to keep sharp.

It is best to hoe when the topmost layer of soil is dryish, as this makes it easier than wet and sticky. A drying day will also help wither the hoed-up weeds, but hoeing in the rain is still better than letting them grow away. A rake afterwards or the next day collects the bigger ones and disturbs any survivors once more. (If used very regularly on clean soil, gravel or fine mulches, then raking can substitute for hoeing.) It was always said: 'if you hoed when you couldn't see a weed, then you never would', meaning that the disturbance of emerging weed seedlings is sufficient to stop them growing further.

Very dense patches of well-established weeds can be heavy going to hoe, in which case it may be better to pre-treat these spots by slicing them off with a sharp spade and taking them away for composting. In much the same way, flushes of seedling weeds can be lifted and inverted in situ with a thin slice of soil using a razor-sharp spade, and this kills them even more effectively than being hoed.

Top left: Pulling a sharper edge onto a hoe blade **Top right:** Swan-necked draw hoe cuts as it's pulled through weeds **Bottom left:** Dutch chisel-like hoe cuts as it's pushed through weeds **Bottom right:** Gloves protect from blisters, note bucket for stones

Hoeing mulches – In stony or very sticky soil hoeing can be difficult, but it can be made easier by raking the soil level then topping it off with a thin layer of sieved topsoil, potting compost or even sharp sand. This allows the area to be more readily hoed. Fine mulches, sand and gravel can all be hoed, but coarse or fibrous ones are more difficult. Ideally, coarse mulches should not be put where weeds are likely to need hoeing as, if they get seeded onto, they can be very hard to hoe. Hand weeding or inversion of the topmost layer with a spade is then more effective.

An unusual opportunity to hoe is in stone-free soil after a hard frost when the ground is frozen solid. At some point the ground remains hard whilst the topmost layer becomes defrosted, thus the weeds are held locked by their roots and right then a hoe can be used most effectively.

Coring and depressing – One less common way of removing weeds, especially suited to those in turf, is with an adapted coring tool (used for aerating turf). A metal tube with a foot bar is pressed down onto and around the weed, which is lifted out so its roots are removed with a core of soil. Alternatively, weeds can be pushed many inches into the ground by a heavy crowbar and the hole filled in above it with soil, sand or compost.

Left: A thick layer of sieved compost will feed the soil, and will be easier to hoe or rake clean than the rougher soil underneath

Dig or fork and pick – digging over – This is the 'traditional' way to clear a bed or border of weeds. Starting at one end, the area is methodically dug over and all weeds removed by hand. If it has well-established weeds, the top growth should first be removed, burnt or composted, then the topmost layer of soil and the weed roots may be skimmed off and stacked to rot down, thus removing the bulk of most weeds. If no difficult weeds, such as stinging nettles or bindweed, are present and the top layer of soil is more like a turf or a green manure, this skimmed portion could be buried at the bottom of each trench as you dig, with clean, picked over soil placed over it. But there is the risk that some weeds might survive, so usually composting the skim separately is preferable. There may be too much material for the average compost heap to take with so much soil attached. If so, rot the skimmed 'turves' in a pile, sprinkling them with lime (unless intended for acid-loving plants), build this into a squat thick wall and cover it with black plastic or anything else which is light-excluding. In a few months, it will have broken down to a fibrous loam suitable for adding to potting compost, enriching poor sites or for giving back to the soil it came from. If the weeds are few, young and not pernicious they may even be dug in as you go, but again, this is risking some surviving. In most cases the soil underneath is dug and broken up, sod by sod, one spit at a time, with all weed roots picked out as you go. A digging fork is maybe better for this than a spade, as each chunk should be lifted up, inverted, thrown down and then smashed to bits, not chopped.

Digging smaller chunks makes for easier and much more effective work; with big bites it's too easy for some weed roots to get reburied unseen.

Throw any roots straight into a barrow, bucket or trug, and have another receptacle ready for stones, and a third for debris such as plastic, metal and glass. The roots collected are probably best soaked in a butt of water for a month or two before adding to the compost bin, because from any depth they are likely to be from tough weeds such as docks, thistles and bindweed. Slow hard work this may be, but it's effective at clearing weedy areas efficiently.

Right: This cold frame developed a good mat of weeds – but all easily removed for compost

Making a new bed or border via turf – This is a slower but very effective way of clearing an area. First, the area is levelled and put down to turf (just mowed regularly), as it will be easy to eliminate almost all weeds with regular mowing over a year or two. Later the turf is removed, leaving very clean conditions. This is worth doing when recovering land covered in dense stands of very tough weeds, such as brambles or stinging nettles. First clear any shrubby top growth, pull up any stumps and compost the bulk of soft growth. Remove junk, such as bricks, wires, etc., then run a rough, strong rotary mower over it every week from early spring and soon most weeds are gone. The result of a succession of cuts is that plants that can endure close cutting, such as grasses, replace weedier weeds, such as nettles and so on, which cannot.

In sun and light shade, grasses usually take over and you soon have a rough sward or turf. (In heavy shade, ivy or another 'weed' may be the more successful ground-covering plant and is probably better retained than removed. Keep this weeded by cutting off the top growth of other weeds emerging above the ivy using a nylon line trimmer or shears.) To speed up the replacement of weeds by grasses you can over-sow in spring or autumn with grass and clover seed. (The latter will fix nitrogen and enrich the soil.) Almost all weeds cannot take regular weekly cutting by a mower, which removes their top growth throughout a whole growing season and so, eventually, their root systems are exhausted, they die and grass fills their place. Of course, a few rosette and creeping weeds survive in the turf but these are removed later with the turf. Soon all the really pernicious weeds have been turned into clippings added back to the soil or rotted elsewhere. Then the grassy turf and top layer of soil can be lifted off with a sharp spade and the area dug over as explained before. The soil spending a year or more as turf in this way makes the actual hand eviction of roots a much less arduous occupation, and also enriches the soil where the clippings are returned.

Left: A piece of turfed ground is easily
and quickly converted into weed-free soil

Weeding ways sitting down

The slower but more effortless way of clearing ground is to kill the weeds by stopping them seeing any light. This can be with plastic sheet, ground-cover fabric, cardboard and newspaper, old carpets, or what have you. Simply cover the weeds and they turn yellow and die. They produce more shoots and leaves; these yellow and die, get eaten by the soil life and, slowly, the surface becomes covered in worm casts. It helps to have a perimeter trench a foot or so deep and wide into which the cover hangs; this prevents weeds near the edge of it surviving from outlying roots. If any weeds find a hole and come through the covering they must be pulled or pushed back under and the spot repaired. (A stone or brick on top may do, or a newspaper placed underneath the covering and blocking the hole will work well.) The best time to cover ground is from late winter, then the weeds die in the flush of spring and are soon incorporated. Muck or compost can be spread beforehand and will be incorporated simultaneously. Such covers can also be applied on top of flushes of weeds or over green manures and are much less effort than hoeing or digging them in. During the growing season, most small weeds are killed in a few weeks and the covering can be removed and used elsewhere.

Black plastic sheet – This does not kill all weeds well unless it is thick enough to exclude all light. Hold it up to the sun, does it show through? If so, use a double or triple layer or lay the sheet on top of newspaper, cardboard or other light-excluding mulch. It works so well as it also heats up the soil, increasing the rate of growth and breakdown of weeds and it keeps the moisture in all the way to the surface, also promoting growth and breakdown. However, the sheet can lift or blow about so it needs tying or weighting down carefully. I find giant pins made from bicycle spokes or cut out of wire coat hangers handy for pinning down such short-term coverings, but for wind resistance little beats holding it down with cast-iron guttering or scaffolding poles. Plastic sheet on uneven ground pools rainwater and channels it to the

Left: Ground-cover fabric does a good job
– but weeds are determined

lowest point, so it must be laid carefully with that in mind. You can reduce the problem, indeed utilise it, by laying plastic sheet over a raked level, or graded, loose mulch or soil, with depressions to guide the water to just where you want it. Or you can create depressions around plants and fit the plastic about them, then the water will be delivered to them.

White sheet plastic – This is sometimes used to throw up light onto the crops but it does keep the soil a tad cooler. White plastic controls weeds if it is opaque, though it is somewhat slower in action than black plastic, which cooks them at the same time.

Punctured or perforated plastic sheet – This allows water and some air to pass through but, unfortunately, some weeds will find the holes. If you use two layers, the perforations do not align and so it works better, or it can be laid over newspaper or cardboard or a loose mulch if only weak weeds are present.

Woven or felted ground-cover fabric – This is the stuff. Usually this is black, sometimes glossy, and not awfully pretty. However, it is quite acceptable in most productive areas and useful for lining cold frames, under paths and in areas full of pots. Some are just woven, some are more of a fleece; in either case, the heavier and thicker the grade the better. This can clear new ground of almost all established weeds – including even brambles and stinging nettles, though they will push it up unless well fixed! Of course, such weeds need pre-treatment by removing the old top growth and giving the area a cut or two with a rough tough mower. But then, providing the edges are well fixed down, any weeds enclosed regrow into the dark, are bent down and are killed off – even the toughest. Laid on top of clean soil, it keeps it clear of weeds and, because the air and rain pass through, it keeps the soil apparently much healthier than under black plastic sheet. In ornamental areas it can be covered with thin layers of a coarse mulch, such as bark or gravel, to improve its appearance. This may make more labour in the long run, though, as these can allow weed seeds to germinate and grow if not well policed.

Old carpet – I no longer recommend this as the ground-cover fabrics do the same job. However, old wool and cotton carpets laid upside down did make a good job of killing off most weeds or keeping an area weed free. They rot and are not a permanent solution unless covered with a loose mulch such as bark. Half-natural half-artificial carpets, latex backed or foam backed should never be used as they break up leaving nasty bits, but they are handy for

lining the floor, walls and even the ceiling of your garden shed, and using as floor covering for suppressing weeds in storage areas of the garden. Nylon carpets are very good, though, as they last forever and can be cut into convenient paths and patches; these kill the weeds under them and can be moved as needed. When they get soil stuck on them or weeds grow on them you simply turn them over or hang them up and hose-wash them clean.

Cardboard and newspaper – These are free, break down eventually and need careful weighting or they blow, but they work well and may also be used as reinforcement against tough weeds under black plastic or ground-cover fabric and, usefully, under loose mulches such as compost or bark. The paper or board layer is strong enough to stop many weeds pushing through but it eventually rots. Although it seems newspaper and corrugated cardboard are relatively clean and leave few problems once broken down, it's safer to avoid using glossy, highly coloured cardboard or paper (such as magazines), as these have polluting ingredients.

Above left: Newspapers held down with rings cut from sidewalls of tyres keep this soft fruit weed free if not pretty; **Above right:** Keep the light out and every plant yellows and eventually dies

Solarising/thermal cooking

This is a method that works best in much warmer countries. The idea is to cook the weeds and/or their seeds in situ using solar power. A black plastic sheet is spread on the ground and firmly held in place; this works as before by both excluding light and by warming the soil. The sun is absorbed by the black plastic, which in turn heats the soil underneath, but also acts as a blanket at night, keeping the heat from leaving again. Then you suspend a clear plastic sheet above it on sticks, strings or wires, which is fixed down to the ground all round the sides. This traps the light and heat not absorbed by the black plastic and keeps much more heat in at night. In hot sun, the temperature inside this tent becomes highly elevated, cooking everything within. Unfortunately, in the UK this may not get hot enough to destroy some weed seeds, though it kills most weeds fast enough – however, they would be killed by the lack of light anyway. In the UK, this technique is of most use for pre-heating the soil for tender crops, which then benefit from the weed-free conditions and moisture retention.

Right: Woven ground-cover fabric keeps this pumpkin patch weed free and warmer

Weed exclusion

Self-weeding plants – Some plants keep themselves protected with their own dead leaves; many, for example, hemerocallis, die down plastering their crowns and all round with their papery leaf remains, which seem almost glued in place. Unfortunately, birds usually destroy these natural papery mulches. Comfrey and borage also seem remarkably effective and the latter makes especially good winter cover, also adding significant fertility. Where leaves simply lay thick on the soil surface, they kill weeds by choking out the light, but some are also chemically suppressing seeds from germinating. Evergreen, and especially conifer needles, and the leaves of many aromatic herbs are most effective and make good woodland path coverings. Those plants where the ends of the leaves touch the ground, such as pampas grass, keep weeds from appearing by their constant scraping motion. Many shrubs inadvertently relieve themselves of penetrating weeds by thrashing about in gales. Briars, however, utilise this habit by having hooked thorns which act as ratchets; so their stems are actually jacked up over branches by the shrubs rocking.

Left: Borage is good at discouraging weeds from starting nearby
Right: Comfrey uses its foliage to choke out surrounding plants; the leaves can be usefully mulched about tomatoes or potatoes

Close-growing – Dense stands, especially of fast-growing plants, are rarely troubled by weeds as they leave few places for them to get a toehold. Providing there are no weed roots or similar in a bed to simply regrow, few weeds appear, as they would have to come from seed, which can rarely germinate in the heavy shade of existing plants. Thus, an area crammed full of big evergreens, or even smaller ones, such as heathers or lavenders, stays fairly weed free. An herbaceous bed fares less well, as weeds can get a hold in winter when the leaves have disappeared and, although dense, the majority of herbaceous plants are not tall enough to out-top many weeds. Deciduous shrubs fall in between; being tall, they can leaf and shade out weeds from early in the year, but they fail to stop all and are prey to climbing and scrambling weeds, such as clematis, bryony, ivy, and so on.

Above: Heathers, once well established, effectively stop weeds germinating underneath
Left: Ivy is a persistent offender controlled with regular cutting back

Green manures – These and cover crops keep weeds from establishing by filling all the soil with more competitive and/or more desirable plants. Bare soil soon greens over with weed seedlings, even in winter. However, if a thick-sown broadcast crop of something else grows away first, the weeds can't get going. Most green manures are from agriculture and more suited to being dug under with a plough than a spade. Avoid winter tares and vetches, Hungarian grazing rye and most clovers; these are really tough weeds themselves. The gardener needs easier-to-kill-off and more useful choices, and I recommend miner's lettuce (*Claytonia perfoliata*), corn salad (*Valerianella locusta)* and the poached egg plant (*Limnanthes douglasii*). These are excellent for autumn sowing and winter cover. (The first two are also salad crops.) All are easy to strip off or incorporate in situ and outgrow most weeds caught in them. More permanent perennial cover crops that are good at excluding other weeds are turf grasses, clovers, ivy in shade or almost any low-growing evergreen. Good choices for ornamental areas are *Alchemilla mollis* and most hardy geraniums; in acid areas, the heathers; and in hot dry places, sedums, especially *Sedum spectabile.*

Right: Claytonia (miner's lettuce) seedlings soon outgrow weeds and right through winter

Weed suppression

As mentioned on page 57, few weeds even bother germinating if they are in the shade of other plants. In fact, most seeds need to be in the very topmost layer of soil and/or see a flash of light to germinate. Farmers get considerably less weeds in fields when they plough and harrow (rake) at night – honestly. If you cut off the light, you first weaken and kill established weeds and then stop more coming – hence the effectiveness of sheets of plastic, etc, and also dense planting in weed control.

However, other ways of blocking the light also stop most weed seeds germinating or emerging into the light and may be more attractive or add fertility value to the soil as well. Deep mulches work well, and much, much better than shallow ones. Too shallow mulches even encourage weeds by keeping the topmost layer moist, so help germinate weed seeds not deeply enough

Left to right: A thick layer of compost on the raked soil would be easy to keep raked and/or hoed weed free. Cover it with a layer of newspaper to defeat scratching birds. Cover newspaper with a weed-seed-free mulch such as composted bark. Once raked level this will give weed-free conditions for several seasons

buried with some light getting through. Deeper is always better. The coarser the material, the deeper the mulch needs to be. You can economise: first rake the soil level, optionally lay down a newspaper or cardboard layer, put down fine-grade mulch in a generous layer, then top off with a coarser variety of the same to hold it in place and provide a disturbance layer for birds so they do not dig down into the finer grade and expose the soil. In any case, all mulches need raking and topping up at least annually to keep them clean. A little hand weeding may be needed occasionally and, importantly, nothing should be allowed to seed onto mulches as this will cause problems.

Various materials make good mulches for suppressing weeds from seed:

Composted bark – The finer grades are better; it looks great but may blow around in the wind if dry or if disturbed by birds. This material adds some fertility and considerable humus in the long run when it is eventually incorporated in the soil. It is excellent for ornamental beds and for vegetable beds if it is fine and not too acid. The coarser grades are very good for topping off finer grades in ornamental areas, especially for shrubberies. Coarse composted bark is one of the better path coatings for foot traffic. Uncomposted bark is potentially risky and should not be used.

Sawdust – This has a dangerous risk of containing wood preservatives unless you know where it comes from. Used as mulch where it is mixed into the soil it can rob the plants of nitrogen, so you need to put down a dressing of nitrogenous fertiliser first or keep the soil and mulch apart with a newspaper layer. It makes a light surface at first, darkening as it ages. As a path, though, it scuffs up too much and carries on the feet. Sawdust really ought to be composted first before being used.

Pine needles – Where available in quantity, these are an effective mulch and are especially good around strawberries. They make an excellent path or mulch for ornamental areas. Being acid, and giving off anti-germination chemicals, they are best used under acid lovers such as conifers and evergreens and not on vegetable beds or where seed is to be sown, as their allelopathic exudations stop seeds germinating.

Mushroom waste – This is most economical when bought in bulk as whole truckloads from the factory. It does have some limey residues but, usually, no nasty chemical ones and frequently gives crops of mushrooms for free. It has a blotchy, whitish appearance when weathered, which some people do not like, but generally it's weed-seed free and very effective. Mushroom waste is well suited to the vegetable bed but is also good in most ornamental areas (except near acid lovers) and about fruit trees.

'Mulch as often and as deeply as you can afford, as it will repay you with saved labour and happier plants.'

Left: Leaf-mould around these cuttings will keep them weed free

Straw – This makes an excellent, if odd-looking, weed-suppressing mulch. Prone to blow around when first laid, it does settle and consolidate. Straw can cause nitrogen robbery if mixed into the soil, but laid on top it causes little problem. Straw does have some weed seeds, though, so if you stop adding more it gives an interesting exercise in agricultural weed identification. However, while you maintain deep straw mulches, few weeds will ever get away. Straw mulches are excellent for utilitarian paths, around strawberries, rhubarb and in the orchard and fruit cage, but not attractive enough for ornamental areas. If available cheaply in bales, straw can be laid in slabs, which is the most effective and long-lived way of using it. Loosened and shaken it goes further but does not do such a good job – and blows more! Composted straw is more attractive as a mulch but, in the processing, the volume contracts to almost nothing compared to what you started with. It does not have a lot of fertility value, though it is usefully high in silica.

Hay – Often confused with straw, hay contains infinitely more weed seeds, does not look so good, goes mouldy and rots quickly. It is not recommended as a weed-suppressing mulch, except, possibly, in an orchard situation.

Right: Strawberries are strawed to keep the fruits clean - but it also does a fair job of keeping weeds from germinating

Peat – Not a very good mulch for many reasons but now it is also considered un-PC to use as peat bogs are reckoned important wildlife resources and sinks for carbon dioxide, so its horticultural use is best downplayed for fear of wrath from the cerebrally challenged and it can be saved for burning in power stations.

Leaf-mould – This does contain some weed seeds, mostly of trees and shrubs, but it makes an excellent, if rather quick to disappear, mulch that also provides superb fertility for the plants it is around, whilst suppressing most weeds. It is really good for everything ornamental and cropping – you really can't have too much of it.

Well-rotted manures – Almost all of them make good mulches which improve soil fertility, but most also carry a huge load of weed seeds. Though weed-seed infested, they obviously have their place in productive areas. As mulches, they are better applied extremely well-rotted, and never, ever fresh (which is vile for the plants and us). Once spread, rake it level and finish off with another, cleaner mulch on top (grass clippings are excellent for this). Well-rotted manures will kill off most young weeds they are placed upon, and will also suppress seedling weeds, especially if they are topped off or hoed or raked. Horse manure was always considered THE mulch for a rose bed; cow manure is considered most generally beneficial; pig is rich but most revolting to handle; bird manures are little use as mulches, being too strong, and are better added to compost heaps.

Grass clippings – A surprisingly effective and much under utilised mulch. If applied in a thick mass, the clippings putrefy, smell and ooze. However, if applied regularly in thin layers they are excellent. One of the simplest ways to keep beds weed free is to apply a layer over newspaper or cardboard, then when any weeds appear, dump more clippings on top of them. Do this weekly with every mow and most weeds can be eliminated – for free! They also add to soil fertility considerably.

Right: Grass clipping mulches are excellent for raspberry beds

Compost – Garden compost is often not pretty when applied as a mulch and is always full of weed seeds. If it is part-dried and then sieved, it presents a much better appearance. The weed seedlings are a moot problem; I don't mind, I hoe anyway, and more weed seedlings are just more fertility. It is obviously best reserved for using around vegetables and soft fruits but can be applied with benefit as a weed-suppressing, fertility-enhancing mulch to almost any plants. However, it does need covering with something neater and weed-seed free if it is to be left untended.

Soil – Sieved soil makes an excellent mulch for many reasons, but is itself so full of weed seeds that it cannot be recommended as a means of keeping down weeds. Of course, if steam-sterilised or baked it's a different matter, but it can then only be used on a necessarily small scale, say around valuable plants or crops. It is especially useful for topping off seed drills where it gives the seedlings a weed-free zone.

Coir – This is the fibre from commercial coconut processing but there is debate as to whether this is as 'bad' as peat, as it is desperately needed to be returned to benefit the soil in the country of production rather than being exported for our benefit. It is an attractive, fibrous, very, very, long-lasting mulch that works well. Eventually, it will add some fertility.

Cocoa mulch – This is made from the, initially, pleasantly smelling shells of cocoa beans. These mat together to make a good weed-suppressing mulch. The finer grades can be applied first, then the coarser ones. They bond together to form an almost cardboard-like layer that works very well, looks pleasant and, when it breaks down, adds a lot of nutrient value to the soil. It also stops slugs getting to your plants as they don't like crossing it. It is not very long-lasting, though, unless annually topped up and is the most expensive option but superb for, say, bedding displays or keeping a bed of hostas both weed and slug free. Cocoa mulch is excellent against weeds around vegetables prone to slugs, as it stays in place well once watered and is a good soil enricher when incorporated later.

Right: A compost/newspaper/cocoa mulch sandwich helps the new tree get away

Shredded paper is free, effective and not nasty once weathered

Shredded paper – A free, effective mulch, this needs to be watered as soon as laid, but then it stays in place. It is not pretty, but it is a good weed-suppressing mulch for fruit cages and around trees and shrubs. Shredded paper will not stop established creeping or strong weeds unless it is immensely deep, but it does suppress weak ones and seedlings.

Potting and sowing composts and growing bags (fresh and used) – These are all weed-seed-free materials. They make good mulches for keeping clean soil free of weeds and are attractively dark. These are especially useful for covering seed drills and for surrounding new and small transplants in the edible or ornamental garden. These composts seriously improve the soil but are too expensive for widespread use and are best reserved for your most important areas of the garden.

Gravel mulches, well laid and maintained, are beautiful and effective

Sand – Not often considered as a mulch, sand is very effective at suppressing weed seeds and can be used to great advantage in asparagus beds, vineyards, rose beds and other situations where light reflected up is of value. It is remarkably cheap, though heavy, and the soil does need raking very level before you apply it. Sharp sand is grittier than smooth or builders' sand and is preferable, and also best for mixing into composts for potting or sowing.

Gravel – This is more problematic to incorporate into the soil if no longer wanted as a mulch. Placed on top of ground-cover fabrics, as is often done for such as courtyard gardens, it's a neat starting point and ensures few future weed problems. Finer grades prevent weeds better than coarser ones and are easier to rake. A deeper layer is best and is also easier to keep raked and clean of weeds.

Stepping stones – These are not often thought of as a method of weed control, however, they are worth considering for a large bed. At times, you will need to step on the soil to hoe or weed, prune, deadhead or just pick flowers or crops and this will pack down the soil or mulch and provide firm spots that are easier for weeds to get away in than a loose surface. Instead, you invest in a load of the cheapest, small concrete slabs, say, one-foot-square ones, and place these between the plants, aesthetically and conveniently, to act as access. Every single one is a bit of bed that will never need weeding again, and they will help keep the soil moist. Then, as the plants grow up, they disappear from view. You could get coloured ones the same shade as a mulch used with them.

Loose sheet mulches – One big objection to these, especially next to lawns, is that birds kick loose mulch materials used to suppress weeds in the border out onto the turf. The answers are to add a small, raised, plastic, wood or aluminium edging to separate the two areas, or a mowing edge (set in slabs, this smooth surface allows the debris to be easily brushed back). Net down the loose mulch along the exposed edge, or use fine mulches that will only benefit the turf and not impede mowing.

Right: For access and to maintain, this is too fussy; better reset as three or four close together, one comfortable pace from the next set

Drill fills and seed covering – When sowing seed in garden soil there are, inevitably, weeds germinating alongside and choking them, and especially as many weeds are quick to germinate. One way to avoid this is to fill the drill or sowing hole with a weed-seed-free material such as sowing or potting compost or sterilised soil. This will ensure few weeds close to the emerging seedlings, and if the compost is a different colour it will also make hoeing other weeds nearby easier before the seedlings emerge and can be spotted. This technique is particularly handy with parsnips, which are notoriously slow to appear. Such a material also prevents capping, which is when the soil turns to a crust over the seed and prevents it emerging. With small areas or when time is precious, maintaining a weed-free layer on top of your soil makes a lot of sense. Carefully part this layer to sow and plant, then replace the material and top up. When broadcast sowing seeds for, say, a drift of flowers or a band of radishes or carrots, you always get weed seedlings mixed in and needing extricating. So first rake level, then apply a layer of sowing or old potting compost or growing bag contents. Water this, then sow onto it. Now top off with another layer of sowing compost all over and tamp down gently but firmly. This will give nearly 100 per cent weed-free results and will save a lot of work later.

Double layers in pots and containers – Many of us may economise on purchased potting compost by using sieved garden compost, mole hill soil, leaf-mould, rotted down turves, and so on, to augment or replace the weed-seed-free commercial product, especially in larger planters. The result is weeds choking our treasures. The answer is simple – just economise on only the bottom three-quarters and make the topmost third or quarter the seed-free commercial stuff.

Left: Well, in theory, the drill fill should have given a better stand of seedlings with few weeds nearby, not this - it's just because the soil is so prone to capping that there are almost no weeds anywhere else

Weedkillers

Actual herbicides are banned under organic regulations, however, there are some marginal cases and 'least bad' choices. Herbicides, as mentioned on page 26, are banned because they do not just kill plants but damage other soil life as well. Some substances do less damage than others and deserve mention, even though they may not be legally available to the amateur in the UK.

Salts, soaps and oils – Some of the original weedkillers were simply strong salts. These kill mostly by sucking the water out of the weeds. Ordinary table salt is very good at this if applied dry onto weeds. Some people have used strong salt solutions to kill seedling weeds and suppress seeds germinating on asparagus beds (asparagus, seakale and beetroot are somewhat salt tolerant, coming from seaside ancestors). Ordinary chemical fertiliser is a very effective weedkiller if applied neat, and although not organic, it eventually bestows some benefit to the soil. A heavy dressing of wood ashes will stick to dew-moistened leaves and choke them, dispatching small and weakening bigger weeds. Amazingly, a spoonful of sugar on top of a wet weed can kill almost as well as an herbicide.

Soap and detergent solutions – These can kill weeds by stripping off the waxy coating so the wind and sun can parch them dry. Obviously, many weeds then regrow from their roots and require a second or third treatment. None the less, this is a cheap, effective method for the smaller, weaker weeds in the middle of summer. In very hot, dry weather, this is remarkably effective.

Acetic acid – Vinegar has been used as an herbicide, though it's only strong enough to kill seedlings; stronger forms are able to kill bigger weeds but need handling with great care. It works in two ways: it strips off the waxy coating, and it also changes the pH – being strongly acidic, it disrupts the internal processes of some weeds.

Oils – Coating the leaves of weeds with various oils can kill the plants by soaking them and, thus, interfering with internal processes and by blocking the airflow, preventing effective transpiration and photosynthesis and so starving the weeds to death. Old frying oil is probably kinder to the environment than mineral-based ones, and research is currently examining different vegetable oils for their effectiveness, particularly cinnamon, citrus, and cloves.

Above: The rest of the boiling water from making a cuppa can go to broil weeds to death

Corn gluten meal – A dressing of this has been found to prevent many weeds from germinating and emerging. As a natural product it may be acceptable to organic gardeners, and it's also a nitrogenous fertiliser – neat, that.

Boiling water – This is a very simple, relatively safe way of dealing with small numbers of weeds in paths, drives, patios and rockeries. You simply pour it carefully over a weed, which will then change colour (it goes a different green) and the leaves wither away. Tougher weeds require several applications, but die they do. This is best done with the dregs from the kettle every time you boil up for a cuppa. The water drained from boiling vegetables can also be used. It is not worth boiling water especially as this consumes a lot of energy.

Steam, hot air and flames – These are all alternative ways of cooking a plant. Steam delivers more heat more effectively and efficiently than boiling water and a hot steam gun, or even a recycled steam iron, quickly kills the leaves and slender stems of weeds. Several treatments a week or two apart will eliminate most weeds. However, many weed seeds, even on the surface, and certainly within capsules, may survive the short period of heating most will receive. Indeed, I reckon it even stimulates some!

Hot air, or rather very hot air, is also very effective at killing weeds. The leaves parch rapidly and small stems wither. Devices somewhat like turbo-charged hair driers are available for legitimate use as paint strippers or fire lighters. Obviously, these carry risks of both electrical and fire hazard, so I cannot recommend their use, only note that this could be an area for research and future safer products designed for this purpose.

The use of a roaring flame to kill weeds is long established. Originally powered by paraffin, but now often by gas, these are no more than glorified plumbers' blowtorches. The flame should not be yellow but a roaring, near invisible, blue flame that you play over a square foot or more, searing everything it touches instantly. You walk slowly along, carefully passing the flame over the weeds. The idea is to cook them not char them away. Cooking withers them and they then take more resources from out of the roots than for merely replacing a burnt away leaf. Flames are very effective at dealing with flushes of seedling weeds and for keeping large areas of soil, gravel or (moist!) mulches weed free. Some flame-guns come on wheels so you can easily run them along gravel drives and so on. A second application, after a week or so, burns

off the now withered leaves, newly fallen leaves and seeds and thus removes much of the opportunity for future weed problems. (Unfortunately, because these are most effectively used on large open areas at speed, there is little chance of any creatures dwelling on the surface escaping. But as the flame passes by very quickly those underground escape unharmed.) Flame-gunning is also especially useful for creating a weed-free sterilised seed bed. An area to be sown is raked level and allowed to grow a flush of weed seedlings. These are flame-gunned off with little effort. The next flush is treated in the same way. It is unlikely there will be a third flush unless the soil is disturbed, as all seeds likely to germinate have done so. Then a crop or flowers are planted with minimal disturbance, perhaps also with a sterile mulch placed over any newly exposed soil around them. These then grow away without much need for any future weeding. But even more cunningly, if seeds are sown with, say, a germination time of two weeks, then you can flame-gun all weeds with impunity up to day thirteen, leaving a very clean soil for the seedlings to emerge into.

Above: The flame is too hot to see and within a minute the weeds all round are all cooked; the full watering can is a sensible safety measure...

Collecting, composting and finishing off weeds

If weeds are cut or hoed off when tiny, then they can be left on the soil surface and will soon be incorporated. As they get bigger, weeds become more risky to leave, as they may still set seed lying there, but they also become withered and lay around looking untidy. This could be acceptable on a vegetable bed but not in ornamental areas. Thus, there is value in raking after hoeing; this further damages those hoed off and any still rooted, and collects up the casualties for composting.

Surface mulching with weeds is the precise opposite of collecting them up. Weeds are allowed to reach some size but nowhere near being able to set seed, then they are hoed off carefully to leave them covering the soil with a ready made mulch. This is a risky practice that is better suited to some green manure crops than with weeds.

Left: Using the raked-up hoed-off weeds as a green mulch is risky, even after leaving them to dry in the sun, so probably best to rake them up and compst them

Please - Unless you are confident of your composting method, do not put perennial weeds on a compost heap without first desiccating or drowning them.

Desiccation is when weeds are left on top of the soil in drying conditions or, better still, on a concrete path or on a wire netting support to wither and dry out. This finishes off those with stronger potential to regrow, such as nettles, horseradish and docks, but in damper conditions some weed roots may survive many weeks. Also, this method may allow some weeds to finish setting and ripening their seeds.

The old Roman way to kill weeded weeds is to put pernicious weeds, weed roots and weeds in seed into butts of water and other vile liquids. There are no land weeds that can survive weeks under water and most seeds soon waterlog and die. Then the liquid part can be used as a feed or added with the slurry to the compost heap. This does smell a bit so plastic dustbins with lids are sensible. You can have these standing in convenient spots near beds to receive weeds as they are collected.

If you do not want to buy commercial weed-seed-free compost for potting or sowing, then you can steam or bake your own. Small amounts can be cooked in a microwave, larger amounts in a normal oven or on a sheet of metal or in half an oil drum over a small fire. The idea is to steam the material so a cover, constant stirring and remoistening may be needed. A dry soil or compost is too good an insulator for straight heating and will simply burn where it is hottest. Thus well-moistened soil or compost should be heated until it steams, then kept steaming for half an hour or so before being allowed to cool.

Right: After a fortnight or more in here, all weed roots and seeds will be dead and safe to go to the compost bin - and a stinky liquid to wet the bin contents or use as a liquid feed concentrate

Different ways for different places

The various ways we have of controlling weeds are almost all applicable to most situations, but not necessarily as well suited. Each area of the garden is more easily kept weeded by certain measures and often differently to other areas. For example, it may be possible, but not comfortable, to hoe a rockery or conversely to hand-weed a bed of hollies, berberis and pyracanthas....

Above: In the fruit cage a sensible mulch yet, in the front garden, less acceptable

Weed control on vegetable beds

Primarily, large vegetable beds are kept weed free by regular hoeing, while smaller and congested beds can be hand weeded. Mulches are not much employed, though they could be used more. Certainly, grass clipping mulches applied about potatoes keep down weeds most efficiently, feed the crop, retain moisture and keep the new potatoes from seeing daylight and becoming greened. Grass clipping mulches can also be useful under and around brassicas, either side of rows of peas and beans, and about turnips and swedes. However, such loose mulches may make the soil too cool for pumpkins, marrows and their family, and for sweet corn and tomatoes; these are better grown through black plastic mulch, which excludes weeds and also warms the soil. Moveable fabric mulches can be useful for clearing beds of weed seedlings or keeping them clean while awaiting the arrival of crop plants. Green manures are good for keeping weeds down through winter and may be dug in, rotted in situ under plastic sheet or removed and composted. Alternatively, deep mulches of well-rotted manure keep the soil relatively free of weeds through most of the winter – though additionally covering this with a black plastic or fabric sheet does an even better job. Drill fills and mulching with weed-seed-free composts help keep the area immediately next to crop seedlings and plants weed free and should be practised more often. Planting out from cells or pots also keeps the soil empty and easily hoed or weeded for longer into the year. (Once the crops arrive you have to work between them, and avoid disturbing any protection they may require, such as nets or cloches.)

With large areas and a wet season, a flame gun can be useful for creating a cleaner seed bed. Temporarily covering with black plastic or ground-cover fabrics can be used likewise. Rotating crops can help with weed control. Those sorts of weeds able to hide amongst, say, peas are then exposed if they come up the next year amongst brassicas. When root crops follow, these may harbour different weeds but these are, in turn, upset by the loose soil and disturbance with potatoes the year after. The annually changing conditions mean few weeds

are continuously well suited. One area worth noting to save weeding work is the paths: it is not wise to have narrow grass paths between vegetable beds as these provide havens for pests, and worse, and the grass and other weeds continually encroach and need frequent trimming back. Paths of sharp sand, fine composted bark, bare soil or even sawdust are easy to keep raked or hoed. Gravel, less so. Solid concrete is excellent. Temporary paths of heavy-duty ground-cover fabric or nylon carpet are also handy.

Above left: This bryony needs evicting.
Above right: It soon makes an energy store in it's swollen (very poisonous) root

Weed control for herbaceous and asparagus beds

One great advantage of herbaceous and asparagus plants is that all their top growth dies away in winter, leaving the ground between easier to scan and hoe or weed. The crowns can be covered with a mulch of almost anything and the whole area flame-gunned a couple of times and then left undisturbed for a clean following season. Or you can use loose mulches, which suit most herbaceous plants really well, but make asparagus rather late to emerge. These loose mulches can be preceded for economy by first laying down fabric, plastic or newspaper/cardboard strips. Stepping stones are strongly recommended.

Left: Hand weeding with a knife between herbaceous crowns is safer (for them) than hoeing

Weed control with rose and shrub beds

Rose and shrub beds can be kept hoed but not if there are underplantings of bulbs, in which case thick loose mulches are probably the best choice. Thick dressings of well-rotted horse manure are traditional under roses, and if applied after the leaves fall, they will suppress fungal diseases as well as weeds by sealing infective material underneath. A dense ground cover of plants may be a good alternative; lavender is effective under roses in sunnier beds, clovers in shadier ones. A ground-cover fabric with a skim of coarse composted bark is a good option for shrubs, but it does make it awkward to add the extra dressings that roses always require.

Above: Weed control fabric works well under soft fruit, roses and shrubs

Weed control in fruit cages and under soft fruit

Soft fruit revel in a moist rich soil and especially one well mulched with leaf-mould. Compost or well-rotted manure or composted barks are other good choices, straw is excellent, and shredded paper is the cheapest option. Under layers of newspaper or cardboard are useful again, and ground-cover fabrics and plastic sheet also work well. Grapevines prefer white plastic sheet or ground-cover fabric to keep down the weeds and keep the soil warm; placing a skim of stones or gravel on top can throw up light and heat. Hand weeding will be needed amongst raspberries and their kin and these prefer thicker mulches than most other fruits. Strawberries are best grown through fabric skimmed with straw.

Right: The saving of moisture, of weeding and the eventual boost to fertility make mulches so sensible under soft fruit

Weed control in woodland and wild settings

Although these are 'natural' areas, if you do not control plants, such as brambles and stinging nettles, you are likely to find they become impenetrable. Establishing ground cover, such as long grass in sunny parts and ivy in shade, makes a lot of sense. Bluebells can do a good job if densely planted in dappled shade but they may not suppress vigorous weeds. In any case, trim everything that emerges above the desired plants with shears or a nylon line trimmer. Be especially vigilant to cut out brambles and stinging nettles as these will take over. Cut grass with a rough tough mower at least every autumn (after wildflower seeds have been dropped) to prevent brambles and saplings getting away. Paths through shady woodlands can be most suitably made from coarse bark. Grass pathways can be mowed through long grass, leaving everything else for an annual cut. Cut another strip on either side of the path a little higher and less often to remain rough grass which will stop weeds and long grasses flopping over onto the path.

Right: Such a natural combination effectively excludes other plants

Weed control of turf, short and long grass

Generally, you do not really want the standard monocrop; a mixture of grasses, clover and maybe creeping thyme and chamomile is much more interesting and smells lovely. However, certain other plants are not desirable, especially thistles, plantains, buttercups, mosses and veronica speedwells. The first three can be hand weeded with a knife, daisy grubber or corer, or have boiling water carefully drizzled over them. Raising the height of the mower's cut, feeding and liming will usually get rid of most mosses, buttercups and speedwells over a couple of years, by changing the soil conditions. However, this cannot be done with a fine bowling green turf or with nearby acid-loving ericaceous plants. Feeding a lawn, over-sowing with a tougher growing grass seed, more regularly cutting, rolling and scarifying will clean up most turf as, with stronger growing grass, the weeds do not get a look in. Increasing the amount of shade over a lawn will promote mosses and eventually ivy, so keep the area open.

Very close-cut grass is prone to daisies and other weeds sneaking in. Worm casts help weeds by providing germination spots in soil, so these are best collected up or brushed off when dry. Very long grass excludes much else, particularly when it flops over. It will be more effective if fed with nitrogenous fertilisers and cut once in autumn.

One unusual way to weed turf is to station geese on it for a few weeks. They will eat the grass down close, enjoy searching out most weeds, and eradicate buttercups particularly nicely whilst adding fertility.

Prevent weeds and grasses growing from turf paths into beds and borders with plastic, aluminium or wooden edging, or with a properly set stone or brick edge (set in concrete so there are no gaps to encourage weeds), or a well-trimmed deep chamfer. If the turf stands well clear up above the soil surface, fewer intrusions will occur. The edge can be kept trimmed with a nylon line trimmer or shears – a half moon edger removes too much.

Left: Longer grass with wildflowers is greener in many ways - and a good excuse for less mowing...

Weed control on paths, drives, patios and rockeries

Surprisingly, perhaps the neatest solution to controlling weeds on hard surfaces is using boiling water from the kettle (see pages 77–8) whenever you have some left over from making a cuppa. This is remarkably effective when dealing with small numbers of weeds in cracks of paths and patios and can be used similarly to cook individual weeds on a rockery. Weeds can also be raked out of cracks with a hook-shaped knife, or sliced out or trimmed off. A more permanent solution is to clean out the cracks and fill them with mortar, cement or mastic, or to fill them with sowing compost mixed with seeds of thyme and chamomile, or maybe dianthus, sedums and sempervivums where there is little traffic. If these fill all available space, weeds can't get in.

A flame gun is good for keeping gravel paths and drives clean, especially one with wheels for larger areas. A smaller hobby gas blowtorch is excellent for weeds in cracks, rockery weeds and spot weeding tough weeds in drives and paths. Black plastic or fabric mulches can be used to kill weeds on gravel drives and paths but the worms may then bring too many casts up to the surface, causing other problems. A more permanent solution is to level the existing surface, lay a ground-cover fabric and then cover it with a generous layer of new clean gravel.

One specific weed problem with solid paths and patios of brick, concrete and stone is that they can get slimy with algae or even mosses. These can be steam cleaned or scrubbed off with warm water, detergent and bleach, or dressed with sharp sand then scuffled or brushed vigorously.

Left: This motley crew is already spreading – look at that bitter cress with its myriad pods

Recovering control in a badly infested mixed bed or border

First, you must decide what state the plants themselves are in. They could be in good condition – healthy clumps of herbaceous plants, drifts of bulbs and shapely, not too overgrown, shrubby plants, just invaded by weeds; or they could be in older, more worn-out condition but worth having; or basically they are past it, or not of great value and better replaced entirely or nearly so.

In the first case, hand weed within and around the clumps of herbaceous plants and shrubs. Remove the weedy top growths and compost them. Then use fabric or plastic or newspaper to cover all the weedy ground in between the plants before covering the whole bed with a loose mulch, such as mushroom compost or fine composted bark. Very carefully hand weed weekly every clump and shrub for the next growing season or two. Top up the mulch regularly. Where drifts of bulbs are planted you can use a thick mulch to stop some weeds and hand weed others, or while the bulbs are dormant, use a flame gun or steam to clear the surface.

Where there are some good but several worn-out plants, it may be best to leave only those that cannot be dug and moved, mostly shrubs and trees. Ideally, dig, split and re-plant in autumn into a temporary bed all those plants that are worth having, probably mostly bulbs and herbaceous ones. It is probably also better to take cuttings of such shrubs as buddleia and flowering redcurrants that root easily, and then you can also remove their parents. Next, roughly level the soil, fill if necessary, and apply a ground-cover fabric, fitting it carefully around those plants that have to be left. Cover this with a loose mulch and hand weed regularly in and about the saved plants while the mulch kills all the other weeds and any regrowth from bits of left over plants. The second year, return the moved-out plants to the bed, cutting through the ground-cover fabric to plant them, then replace it with more loose mulch on top and continue to hand weed.

In the worst case scenario, if you have rubbish plants that are well overgrown, the best approach is to dig, split and temporarily plant elsewhere any that are worth replanting. Likewise, take cuttings of good shrubs where possible, then eradicate everything left in the bed. Either dig and pick over the bed as explained earlier (see page 44), then put it all down under a fabric or plastic sheet mulch for a year or two, but really the better option is putting it all down to turf, mowing it for a year or two then cutting a new bed out of the turf and moving back into it all the bulked up plants you've propagated meanwhile.

Left: Sometimes it's simplest just to dig
it over, picking out the weeds as you go

Other uses
for weeds

Food – Many weeds are not only edible but are, or at least were, considered good tucker by some folks. Stinging nettles are excellent, or rather their young tips are when fried with bacon and onions; dandelions, once blanched, are even better. Docks were made into puddings and plants such as chickweed and fat hen were added to the pot. Whole books are devoted to such free fodder but, to be fair, most of them are not that great eating.

Herbal uses – I can't recommend such use in these litigious times, but goosegrass has long been used for cystitis; ground elder was known as Bishop's weed as they took it for gout; and even couch grass and nettles have their advocates. Indeed, almost every weed is alleged to cure something or other.

Chicken and pet food – If you do not want to eat weeds your hens or pets probably will. Hogweed is good for feeding rabbits, hens love to eat chickweed and fat hen (sic) and grass, as do geese which also, of course, relish goosegrass.

A cunning device for converting weeds, seeds and bugs into breakfasts

insect encouragement – Almost every weed is intimately connected with some insect or another and some are their sole suitable source for nectar or pollen. So some weeds should be allowed to grow where they are less of a problem just so their associated insects will be maintained. Of course, of these some will be potential pests, however others will be their control as well. (Weeds that are especially good at feeding a wide range of insects are listed in Appendix IV – see page 110.)

Mineral accumulators – The very properties that make weeds so dangerously competitive with our plants also make them intrinsically useful. As they can find, scavenge and accumulate certain elements to very high levels, even in soils effectively short of them, we can use them as fertilisers. Actually, there is usually plenty of almost every element in the soil; but locked up as insoluble forms so most plants cannot get at them very easily. Whichever element is required can be released and concentrated by a crop of weeds that are good at accumulating it, then these weeds can be dug in, rotted into a liquid feed or composted, before flowering, to release their wealth back into the soil. Say your soil is low in phosphorus, then use thornapple (datura). These are pernicious weeds if grown with a crop, but if not allowed to flower and seed are one of the best accumulators for phosphates. Compost them and return the compost to the soil now it is richer in phosphates and can support a better crop. (See Appendix III on pages 108–9 for those weeds known to accumulate valuable elements.)

Ground cover – As you may have annoyingly noticed, weeds are remarkably good at covering bare soil, winter and summer. Although some come up almost year round, many weeds germinate at different times of the year. Thus, between them, they soon restore nature's green coating, protecting the soil from wind and rain erosion, scavenging nutrients and sunlight that would otherwise be lost. So, although they do need controlling before they become too well established, a flush of weeds is not all bad and there are few green manures as effective. As always, timing is everything; as long as this flush is dug in or taken away and composted then it's just a useful ground cover and green manure crop. In some circumstances, a covering of 'weeds' may be more acceptable, and easier to maintain, than many other options. For example, along the verges of a long country drive it may be better to allow stinging nettles to dominate; these are good for wildlife, exclude almost everything else, can be cut for their rich compost value, if required, and only need a trim once or twice a year to be maintained relatively neatly.

The future of weed control

There is much experimentation into natural herbicides made from plant products. However, as research continues, we can expect to see more novel weed control methods. Many plants give off exudations that prevent germination or affect growth, and the use of these as companion plants or extracts could be very effective. For example, many varieties of wheat, barley and rye give off exudates that hinder the germination of some broad-leaved weeds. More strangely, Timothy grasses use their pollen to prevent nearby plants setting viable seed; just ten grains of their pollen on the stigma of other plants is enough to do this!

Biological controls have proved effective on an agricultural scale in other countries; the opuntia cactus overran much of Australia until a moth was introduced which effectively eliminated it within a few years. We already buy biological controls for many pests, and I suspect it is only a matter of time before we will be offered similar controls for specific weeds. And how about training wood pigeons to eat only brassica-related weeds instead of our cabbages?

Left: Imagine a world where the birds ate only the weeds and caterpillars

Appendix I:
Weed groups

Weeds you want to see in a prospective garden:
masses of stinging nettles!

Other favourable weeds you need not fear: chickweed, forget-me-not,
fat hen, goosegrass, groundsel, thistles, yarrow.

Weeds that are common, very tough, but only require a series of
treatments a week apart to die: brambles, coltsfoot, couch grass,
creeping buttercup, docks, ground elder, knotweed, nettles, thistles,
tree saplings.

Weeds you may be happier not taking on: horseradish, lesser
celandine, oxalis, winter heliotrope, bracken.

Weeds where it may be better to choose another garden: white-
flowered bindweed, equisetum, Japanese knotweed, neighbour's
leylandi hedges.

Weeds in waiting – garden plants that may RAPIDLY become
weeds: alliums, ajugas, alstroemeria, bellflowers, bluebell, brunnera,
celandines, cotoneasters, euphorbias, false valerian, feverfew, forget-
me-not, foxgloves, goldenrod, grape hyacinth, grapevines, Himalayan
balsam, honesty, hypericums, *Iris foetidissima*, ivies, lamiums,
loosestrife, mints, nepeta, oxalis, polemoniums, polygonums, poplars,
pot marigolds, poppies, Russian creeper (*Polygonum baldschuanicum*),
pulmonaria, shasta daisies, sedums, sweet rocket, sisyrinchium,
sycamore, vincas, violas, willows.

'One man's favourite hedge or tree may be a neighbour's hated weed.'

Above left: Ground elder is resilient but eradicable with patience
Above right: Goosegrass and stinging nettles are signs of good soil

Appendix II:
What weeds may indicate

What weeds are telling you is the conditions they like growing in; the very plants most suitable to any given condition are those most likely to be found there. If one type of weed occurs it may be chance, if there are several growing that you know like the same conditions, this is very likely to indicate that you have those conditions. Given time the area will contain the natural 'weeds': the trees, shrubs and other plants suitable to those very conditions. This process will itself change those conditions and thus the vegetation alters further. As leaf-mould builds up, an alkaline soil can eventually become less so – it may even develop an acid layer on top, thus favouring different weeds. This often happens with turf, which can be quite acidic even when overlying a chalky soil.

Weeds that occur most frequently on acid soil: betony, birch, black bindweed, broom, cinquefoil, corn chamomile, cornflower, corn marigold, corn spurrey, daisy, foxglove, fumitory, gorse, harebell, heather, horse- or mare's-tail, lesser periwinkle, mercuries, pansy, rowan, scabious, shepherd's cress, small nettle, Scots pine, sorrels, spurrey, tormentil.

Weeds that prosper on limey soils: agrimony, bell flowers, black medick, briar roses, candytuft, cat's ear, clematis, cornelian cherry, cowslip, dogwood, goat's beard, greater hawkbit, hawthorn, hazel, horseshoe vetch, knapweed, lamb's lettuce, mignonette, ox-eye daisy, penny cress, privet, salad burnet, spindle, stonecrop, tansy, valerian, wallflower, white mustard, wild carrot, yarrow.

Weeds that will thrive in a heavy clay: annual meadow grass, creeping buttercup, cowslip, goosegrass, hoary and ribwort plantain, meadow cranesbill, nipplewort, selfheal, silverweed.

Weeds that like a light dry soil: annual nettle, bramble, broad dock, bulbous buttercup, charlock, dandelion, groundsel, knotgrass, mouse-eared chickweed, stinging nettle, petty spurge, poppies, red dead nettle, rosebay willowherb, shepherd's purse, speedwell.

Weeds that prefer wetter places: alder, bugle, bulrush, buttercup, comfrey, cuckoo flower, dock, hemp agrimony, Himalayan balsam, loosestrife, marsh marigold, meadowsweet, mints, mouse ears, plantains, primrose, ragged robin, sedge, stinging nettle, thistles, water avens, willows, great willowherb.

Above: Red dead nettle in profusion is a sign of a light dry soil

Appendix III:
Mineral values of weeds

These weeds are especially useful as mineral accumulators, so they may be encouraged for this reason, though some (marked*) may potentially cause problems through overwintering pests and diseases.

In general, all these weeds are mostly easy to kill off and collect for compost whilst small, but some may become established and hard to eradicate if allowed to get larger. It is their very competitiveness for their preferred minerals that makes these weeds such bad companions but so good for compost. Weeds such as thornapple will scavenge scarce phosphates from a very poor soil and then, when composted and returned, significantly increase their availability. But. if these weeds are left to ripen seed, the phosphates become locked up in the seeds and so they are no longer available until germinated and gathered as new seedlings or plants.

Chickweed* accumulates copper, iron, manganese, nitrogen, potassium.

Chicory accumulates magnesium, potassium.

Clovers accumulate nitrogen.

Comfrey accumulates potassium.

Corn chamomile accumulates calcium, potassium.

Corn marigold accumulates calcium, phosphorus.

Daisies accumulate calcium, magnesium.

Dandelion accumulates calcium, copper, iron, nitrogen.

Fat hen* accumulates calcium, iron, nitrogen, phosphorus, potassium, sulphur.

Foxgloves accumulate iron.

Goosegrass accumulates calcium, potassium.

Groundsel* accumulates iron, nitrogen.

Plantains* accumulate cobalt, magnesium, potassium, silica.

Purslane accumulates calcium, nitrogen, phosphorus, potassium, sulphur.

Salad burnet accumulates magnesium.

Scarlet pimpernel accumulates calcium.

Sheep's sorrel accumulates phosphorus.

Shepherd's purse* accumulates calcium.

Silverweed accumulates calcium, iron, magnesium.

Sowthistles accumulate copper, nitrogen.

Stinging nettles accumulate iron, silica.

Sun spurge accumulates boron.

Tansy accumulates potassium.

Thistles accumulate potassium.

Thornapple accumulates phosphorus, potassium.

Vetches accumulate cobalt, copper, nitrogen, phosphorus, potassium.

Yarrow accumulates copper, magnesium, nitrogen, phosphorus, potassium.

Far left: A blanket of chickweed is a source of fertile mineral materials
Left: Clover with grass keeps it lusher and greener

Appendix IV:

Weeds known to be especially valuable to insects

Bristly ox tongue, *Picris hieracioides*, visited by at least 27 different insect species.

Dandelion, *Taraxacum officinale*, is a host to predatory wasps and attracts at least 93 different insect species. Unfortunately it also harbours Mangold Fly, *Pegomyia betae*, which may attack turnips and other crops.

Hemp agrimony, *Eupatorium cannabinum*, a weed of damp places which is visited by 18 different insect species, half of which are Lepidoptera.

Hogweed, *Heracleum sphondylium*, flowers visited by 118 species of insect.

Knapweed, *Centaurea jacea/nigra*, visited by at least 48 different insect species, of which more than a dozen were Lepidoptera. Out of every hundred visitors to the flowers, 58 are bees, 27 butterflies and moths, and 12 flies.

Ox-eye daisy, *Chrysanthemum leucanthemum*, visited by 72 different insect species.

Ragwort, *Senecio jacobaea*, is dangerous to stock, causing liver cancer, but beneficial to insects and is visited by 49 different species, predominantly bees and flies.

Rough chervil, *Chaerophyllum temulum*, flowers visited by 23 species of insect.

Thistles, *Cirsium arvense* and others, may be unwanted companions in most places but they're visited by 88 different insect species, including many butterflies.

Vetches, *Vicia* spp., feeding on these aphids is particularly good for ladybirds increasing their fecundity.

Wild chervil, *Anthriscus sylvestris*, flowers visited by 73 species of insect.

Welted thistle, *Carduus acanthoides*, visited by 44 different insect species.

Index